Rookie Read-About Science®

A Snail's Pace

By Al[illegible]wler

Consultants
Linda Cornwell, Learning Resource Consultant,
Indiana Department of Education

Sharyn Fenwick, Elementary Science/Math Specialist,
Gustavus Adolphus College, St. Peter, Minnesota

Janann V. Jenner, Ph.D.

Children's Press®
A Division of Grolier Publishing
New York London Hong Kong Sydney
Danbury, Connecticut

Visit Children's Press® on the Internet at:
http://publishing.grolier.com

Designer: Herman Adler Design Group

Library of Congress Cataloging-in-Publication Data

Fowler, Allan.
A snail's pace / by Allan Fowler.
p. cm. – (Rookie read-about science)
Includes index.
Summary: Briefly describes the physical characteristics of snails and a few of the thousands of species of these creatures that exist.
ISBN 0-516-20812-8 (lib. bdg.) 0-516-26482-6 (pbk.)
1. Snails—Juvenile literature. [1. Snails.] I. Title. II. Series.
QL430.4.F68 1999 97-31280
594'.3—dc21 CIP
AC

Printed in the United States of America
3 4 5 6 7 8 9 10 R 08 07 06 05 04 03 02 01

When people say that something is moving at a snail's pace, they mean very, v-e-r-y s-l-o-w-l-y.

A snail has only one "foot" along the bottom of its body. As the snail crawls, it lets out a slimy goo. The snail slides over the goo by moving the muscles of its foot.

No wonder a snail
moves so slowly!

Most of a snail's body is covered by a hard shell. The snail seems to be carrying its house on its back.

Some people collect these spiral-shaped shells as a hobby.

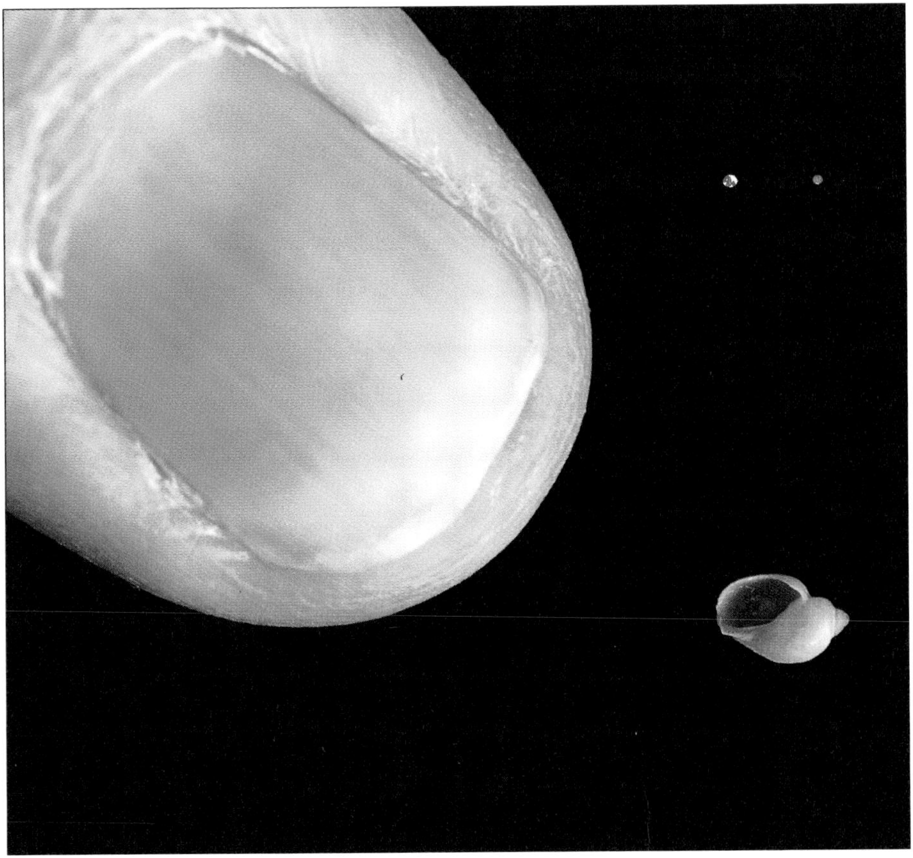

The smallest snails are so tiny that four of them could fit end to end across the letter "m."

The largest snails are about 24 inches (60 centimeters) long.

Sticking up from a snail's head are one or two pairs of tentacles, or feelers.

Most land snails have two pairs of tentacles.

Their eyes are on the ends of the longer pair.

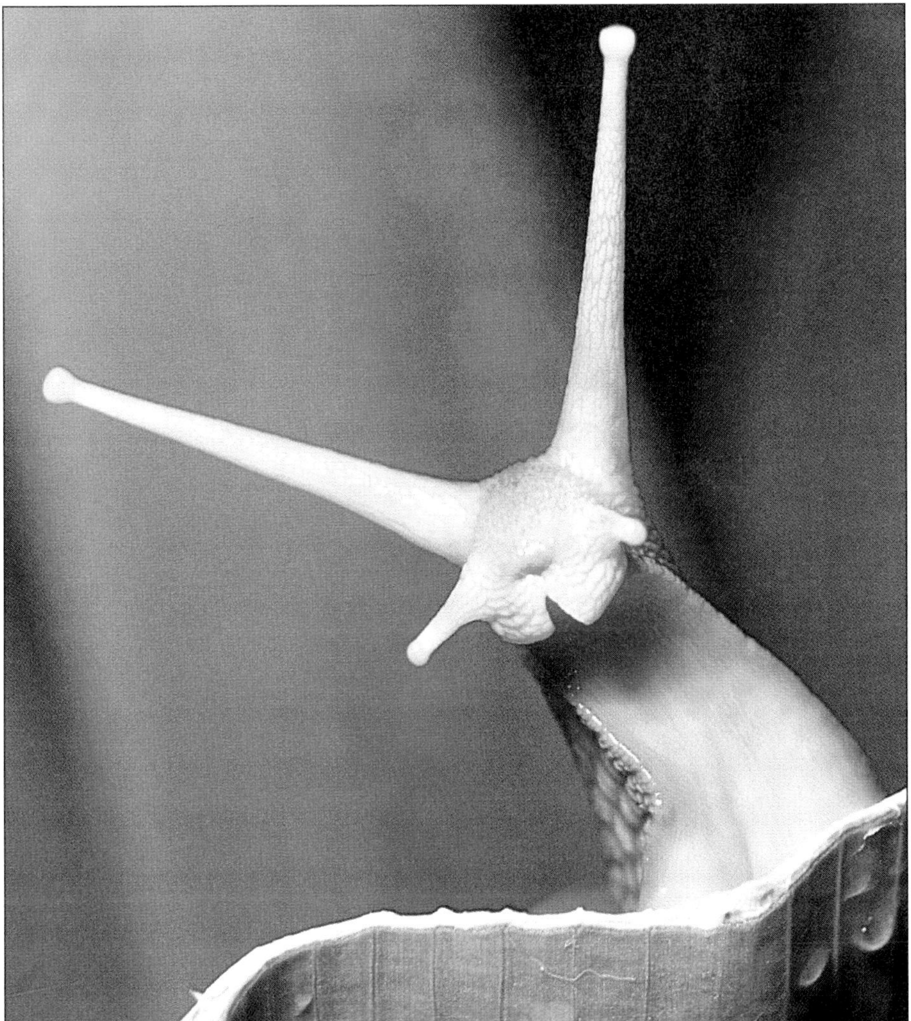

There are thousands of different kinds of snails.

Land snails live on the ground or in trees.

Water snails live
in freshwater, such
as rivers or ponds.

They also live in
saltwater oceans.

Land snails have
lungs for breathing.

Most saltwater, and some freshwater, snails breathe like fish, through gills.

Snails eat mostly plants.

Slugs do, too.

Slugs are members of the snail family, but they don't have shells.

A big slug may be 6 inches (15 cm) long, and a small one may be less than 1 inch (2.5 cm).

Most slugs live
on land, but there
are also sea slugs.

Slugs may move at a snail's pace, but they can do great damage to a garden in a very short time.

At night they come out of their hiding places to nibble on plants.

Do you think snails would be good to eat? A lot of people enjoy them. Never eat a snail that you catch yourself.

The snails served in restaurants are specially raised to be safe and tasty. French restaurants call snails *escargots* (ess-car-GO).

Maybe they're afraid some people won't order them if they know the word escargots means snails!

Words You Know

escargots

shells

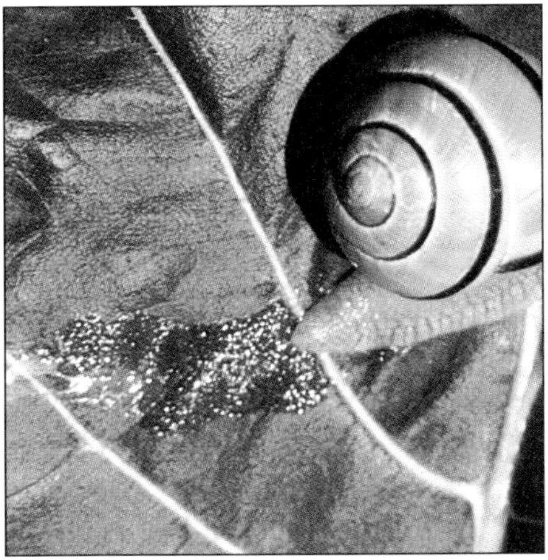
slimy goo

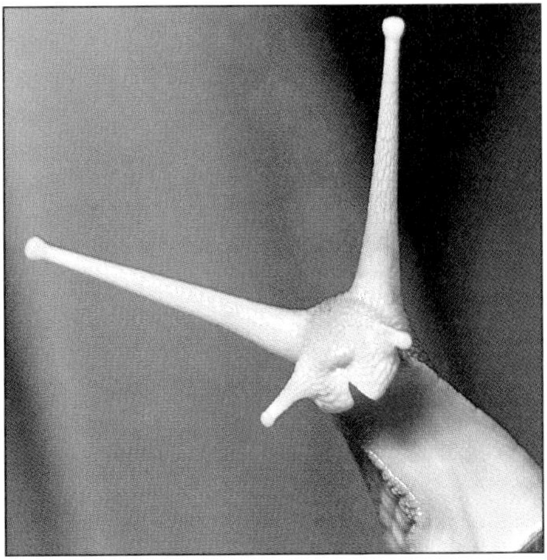
tentacles

land snail

water snails

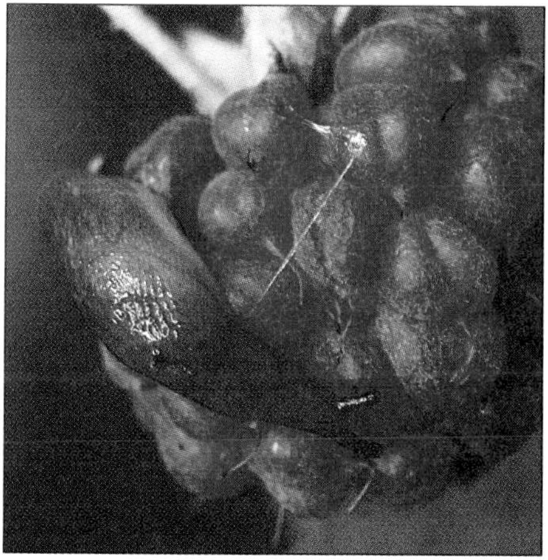

slug

sea slug

Index

About the Author

Allan Fowler is a freelance writer with a background in advertising. Born in New York, he now lives in Chicago and enjoys traveling.

Photo Credits

©: Envision: 27, 30 top left; James P. Rowan: 16; Photo Researchers: 5 (Leland Brun), 29 (Joseph T. Collins), 7, 30 top right (Treat Davidson), 11, 30 bottom right (Fred McConnaughey), 4, 30 bottom left (Yva Momatiuk), 8 (William H. Mullins), cover (L. West), 17; Visuals Unlimited: 18 (Joel Arrington), 21 (D. Cavagnaro), 12, 31 top left (Robert Clay), 3 (Mary Cummins), 14, 31 top right (John D. Cunningham), 23 bottom, 31 bottom right (Dave B. Fleetham), 23 top (A. Kerstitch), 20 (Joe McDonald), 13 (Gary Meslaros), 24 (Glenn M. Oliver), 26 (Charles Preitner), 19, 31 bottom left, 6 (William J. Webber).